I Held My Mother's Pain

A Journey of Healing,
Remembering, and Honoring
The Inner Child

TAYLOR KINNEY

BALBOA.PRESS
A DIVISION OF HAY HOUSE

Balboa Press books may be ordered through booksellers or by contacting:

Balboa Press
A Division of Hay House
1663 Liberty Drive
Bloomington, IN 47403
www.balboapress.com
844-682-1282

Because of the dynamic nature of the Internet, any web addresses or links contained in this book may have changed since publication and may no longer be valid. The views expressed in this work are solely those of the author and do not necessarily reflect the views of the publisher, and the publisher hereby disclaims any responsibility for them.

The author of this book does not dispense medical advice or prescribe the use of any technique as a form of treatment for physical, emotional, or medical problems without the advice of a physician, either directly or indirectly. The intent of the author is only to offer information of a general nature to help you in your quest for emotional and spiritual well-being. In the event you use any of the information in this book for yourself, which is your constitutional right, the author and the publisher assume no responsibility for your actions.

Any people depicted in stock imagery provided by Getty Images are models, and such images are being used for illustrative purposes only. Certain stock imagery © Getty Images.

Print information available on the last page.

ISBN: 979-8-7652-5404-2 (sc)
ISBN: 979-8-7652-5403-5 (e)

Library of Congress Control Number: 2024919028

Balboa Press rev. date: 09/30/2024

The pain in these poems has been held tightly for generations in my maternal lineage. The women who came before me had their own stories that were left untold as they held and passed on the wounds from their mothers of generations prior.

To the women in my lineage,

I see you.
I hear you.
This pain will no longer live inside my body.
I forgive and honor all that came before me.

Part I

Heart, Air, and Fire

My mom dying changed my life.
And it wasn't because I was still so young.

It was the way she died.

She held onto her pain, most times discharging it.
She also handed it to me.

I had been watching her slowly die since the day I was born,
Keeping secrets, walking outside her truth.

I was curious if she ever let herself live.

This unraveling catalyzed a fire in me that I couldn't deny,
No matter how much I wanted to.
I always felt different living in that house,

An outsider looking in, wondering why it had to be this way.

As the years move forward, clarity continues to find me in new ways,
Mostly through words, travel, and a whole lot of self-love.

I'm still learning how to honor this process,

How to honor myself, my body, and most importantly, my spirit.
She's relentless, and I am grateful for her above all else.

Some of these poems express deep sadness, pain,
And years of generational trauma.
Some of these poems speak of love, kindness,
And magical moments deeply imprinted in my soul.
The words on these pages have allowed for breath inside my body.

I hope these words provide resonance,
Maybe even an exhale,
Inspiration to step forward in a new direction,
With space to be held and seen.

Capacity

I pushed her away time and time again
Until she started to haunt me.

I was inventive, innovative.
I was waiting for that story to come.
But this one kept whispering, "This one first."

I fought with her; I pleaded, "No."
She held her ground,
Fighting back with me,
Demanding expression.

The truth—
She is gentle.

In her gentleness, she clarified,
"My love, you are afraid,"
Her words resonating.

I met fear in utero,
Her grip ever so binding.
She overpowered my little body.

At the time, it was the only way.

I adapted to run with her.
Pulsing, she gave me fuel,
Determination.
I was up for every challenge.

Until the day came,
My body
Sounding the final alarm.

Her wisdom screamed,
"See me, Taylor.
Sit with me; be with me."

My capacity only allowed visiting her in bites.
The descent would take me all the way down

Every time.

"Slow and steady," Truth whispered.
My body knew the way.
She was searching for a safe place.

She needed time, space,

To hear, to see, to feel,

To let go.

With each release, an expansion was created,
More capacity for breath, for life, and most
importantly,

For love.

A Girl on Her Own Time

I arrived three weeks early.
My mother in labor, her best friend from high school, a bathtub, and a pickup truck.

My mother's second and last child, baby sister to her first daughter, three years older than me.

My grandmother shared on more than one occasion that my father found out of my arrival via a sign in the teachers' lounge welcoming my birth.

This sign was kept in a box underneath the stairs in my childhood home.
I held it in my hands the month after my mother died,
Me crouched in the tiny storage area,
Sifting through all that my mother held onto.
"This the one?" I said, holding it up to my grandmother as she passed by the doorway.
She chuckled in confirmation.
If passive-aggressive were rightfully defined,
My grandmother's name would be listed as an example.

Fairy Godmothers

I gently placed a gold circle around her.
She looked up at me,
Her eyes filled with relief,
The gold light shimmering all around,

Back in its rightful place.

I spoke softly.
Her words were just starting to form.

"This gold circle will remain around you.
In time you will see
I have always been with you,
My love.

"Thou mayest it be."

The Masculine

Absence.
Present for your students.
I was waiting on the front steps,
Picking at my shoelaces.
Mom helped me take off my jacket.
She said you had a change of plans.

You loved receiving admiration,
Attention, and praise too.
Couldn't you see
Your youngest daughter
So desperate
To receive love from you?

This year I blew out my birthday candles.
I turned four the third week in May.
Did you know what I so badly wished for
Was for you to hold me and tell me you would
stay?

Connections

I was a toddler when I received my first message.
My mother and I were standing at my bedroom door.
I was looking up at her, sobbing.
She was telling me I had to stay in my bedroom.

Pleading with her, I heard a clear voice from a distance say,

"Go back to your own bed; we are protecting you."

I paused, catching my breath and wiping my face.
My mother tilted her head to the side, looking at me confused.
I nodded my head and walked back to my bed to sleep for the night.

I hit play on my cassette tape.
Kathie Lee Gifford's "Dreamship" started to play.

Crawling into bed, I listened to her sing about the dolphins.
I wondered why my mom didn't know about the dolphins.

I wished so badly she did.

Grasping

I held my mother's pain,
Her fears, her harsh words, and her judgment.
She was volatile.
When I spoke up, she distanced herself.

Just be quiet, I said to myself.
No! Another part of me fought back.

She picked me up to dance with me when I was
three.
Finally! I thought. *She sees me.*
My sister called for her in the next room.

She set me back down.
The moment came and went.

What's wrong with me? I wondered.
*Why doesn't she want more moments like this
with me?*
"It's OK," I whispered to myself.

"Maybe she will come back."

Risers and My Favorite White Socks with the Lace Ruffles

I was graduating four-year-old preschool,
Standing on the risers in my classroom,
My peers surrounding me,
A white paper cap sitting on the top of my head.
It was time to sing, my teacher said.
I looked into the audience.

He was there,
Sitting with my grandmother and my mother.

My heart racing, my stomach queasy,
I closed my little legs tight together,
Desperately wanting pants to cover me.

Why did she have to put me in this skirt?
Sing, I said to myself. *Just sing.*
I looked around and down at my shoes.
I noticed my white socks with the lace ruffles.

They made me smile inside.

The sound of clapping—the ceremony was
ending.

We passed the audience in a single-file line.
"Not here. Please not here," I whispered to myself,
My body tightening.
I held my breath passing him
And followed my classmates out the door.

My Therapist Judy

I was around five years old when I met my first therapist.
Her name was Judy.
I was in Judy's office because I had told my mother that my grandfather was giving me orgasms.

This happened for several years.

I delivered this message to my mother while standing near the master bedroom of my grandparents' newly custom-built home.

My grandmother had dreamed of that home her whole life,
The golf course, the three-car garage, the Jacuzzi tub with a fireplace in the master bedroom.
My mother's face was blank.

Somewhere between that day and the day I entered Judy's office, it was decided I would attend therapy.

That day marked the beginning of my journey in therapy,

Attempting to understand the people and the world around me.

Toilet Seats

She was facing me, holding a cup of warm water.
My private parts burned; I had to pee very bad.

My little arms were shaking.
I could hardly hold myself up on the toilet seat.
I wanted to cry so bad.

I don't trust you, I said to her inside my head.
Her body language communicated irritation.
She poured the water down the front of my pelvis.
I released my pee,
Feeling sharp pain shooting through my entire bottom.
I started crying.

When it was over, I looked at her,
Knowing,
I am not safe here with you.

I recalled the exam table, the giant green stuffed frog behind me

And the nurse in front of me asking if I wanted to watch what she was doing on the video screen.
"No," I told her, afraid for my whole life.
She began the exam, and as I started to fight back,

My mother came over and held me down.

I blacked out.

When I woke up,
I could hardly walk,
Wondering if there would be more exams.
They asked me if I wanted to take a Beanie Baby home with me.
I thought, *Is this what I get for speaking up?*

I don't ever want to speak up again.

Back in the bathroom,
I pulled up my underwear, feeling my entire insides burn.
I wondered if my body would burn permanently.

I was too scared to ask.

Justice?

A lawsuit occurred after my disclosure.
I received a sum of money equivalent to the cost
of a semester at the local college for enduring
those experiences.
When I found out about this money,
My heart caved in.

What I needed was his protection and love.
His presence, his time, and his affection.

I encountered this generosity again in the weeks
that followed my mother's death.
I received a text message informing me he was
no longer keeping me on his health insurance
plan unless I paid him a monthly fee.

I reminded him that he was insured on a family
plan,
Also, insuring his son,
Who was three years younger than me.

A few weeks later,
I was notified by the insurance company that I no longer had health insurance.

I thought his timing was impeccable, and I was curious if my mother was rolling over in her grave.

They Say It Happens in Threes

I was standing on the landing next to the front
door,
My mother and I about to head out for an errand.
I was around seven years old.
I shared with her that her friend's daughter had
been inappropriate with me while playing house.

She stared at me for a minute in silence.

I asked if I would have to go see Judy again.
She quickly replied, "No," and told me she would
speak to her friend about it.

Confused, I said, "OK," and followed her out
the door.

Seven of Swords

I told my mom she was a liar.

I was eight years old, standing in the garage.
She had a big reaction to my statement,
One filled with volume and disgust as she glared
back at me.

She protested, "I am not a liar."

I looked at her, noticing her behavior.
I wondered,
*Does she know her words and behavior never
seem to match?*
I replied to her inside my head and giggled:

You are definitely a liar.

Pretenders

I was nine years old, walking up to home plate.
Before I stepped into the batter's box,
I looked behind the home plate fence.
My grandmother, grandfather, and mother were
all sitting behind home plate together.

What is he doing here? I wondered.

I stopped going to the shop years ago after I
had told.
My mother continued to work with him every day.

They ran the family business together,
A betrayal I wouldn't fully grasp until years later.

I saw the three of them sitting together,
And in that moment I realized,

It hadn't only happened to me.

It happened to my grandmother.
It happened to my mother.
They were all pretending.

I glanced down at my cleats,
Black with a white Nike swoosh on the side.
Oh, I'm supposed to be up to bat.

I quickly shoved all my thoughts and knowings
away and stepped into the batter's box.

"I'm ready," I said to the umpire.

Dear Mom

You could never go anywhere without your red
lipstick.
I watched you reapply it in the bathroom mirror—
The rearview mirror too—
One side and then the other,
Smudging your top lip and bottom lip together,
Dipping your pointer finger in the middle.

That red lipstick was your signature.

Your toes were painted the same color,
A deep burgundy red,
The only color you ever wore.

I chose the same color for years,
I wanted to be just like you.
I played ball because you loved it.
I wanted you to love me too.

Did you know that what I really wanted was to
play piano?

I could feel the music.
My hands connected to the vibrations.

How come you never asked?
It was only when I followed you
That I received a glimpse of your love at last.

Out of the Closet

I was ten years old when I outed my mother's sexuality.
A few years had passed with her spending time with one specific friend.

She would sleep over at the house.

When I inquired about my mother's sleepovers, her response was,
"Well, don't your friends sleep with you when they sleep over?"

I thought, *What an interesting way around this conversation.*

I expressed that I was uncomfortable with her friend sleeping over.
She reassured me that her friend would no longer be spending the night.

To confirm her words, I would sneak into my mother's room in the middle of the night to check the other side of the bed.

Her friend was still there.
I even touched her hair once to make sure my eyes were seeing correctly.

One day when my mother was out of the house, I snuck into her room and started searching her dresser drawers.

I found pornographic photos of her friend inside a card.

My stomach dropped; I sucked in my breath.

Waiting until my mother arrived home with my sister and grandmother,
I stood at the top of the staircase facing the front door.
I held the card and photos up in my right hand.

My voice shaky, I said,

"So, are we going to talk about this?"
My mother's face was blank.

I started crying.
My grandmother, sincerely out of the loop, asked what was wrong.

My throat felt like cotton balls and needles as I shared,
"Mom is a liar, and she's also gay."
My mother's entire demeanor shifted during the family meeting that occurred in the living room after this disclosure.
I had never seen her behave like this before.
As I was observing her,
It was in that moment that I realized she wore many masks.

My entire being was in shock during this meeting. My inner knowing receiving the confirmation that my mother had indeed been gaslighting me for years.

Probably my whole life.

I was also beginning to wonder what else she was lying about.
She put a lock on her bedroom door after this meeting.

It seemed truth lived in a faraway land and nowhere inside the house I was living in.

Seven of Cups

It was approaching midnight.
I looked around,
And seeing that no one seemed to be in the
house,
I stepped into the garage.

My body froze.
I held my breath.

My mother was sitting on the garage step,
sobbing.
I looked out into the driveway.
Her girlfriend at the time was standing next to
her vehicle.
The SUV was running with the lights on,
The car door open.

I asked my mother what was wrong.
She said,

"She's making me choose. And I can't.
I'm just going to kill myself."

Caught off guard, I questioned,
"Choose what?"
Her voice filled with despair, she replied softly,
"Between her and my kids,"

My stomach tightened; my heart sank.

I turned to grab the handle of the door to walk
back inside.
I didn't know it was ever a choice, I thought.

Tethers

I wanted to run from you
And run to you,
Your womb
Rattling,
Sensing the unease.
You told stories of birthing me,
Delight, as you grasped my newborn body
Reaching from your vaginal canal.
I am from you,
Don't you see?
Resting safely in your presence
Is the only place I ever longed to be.

House of Cards

We were visiting my grandmother for the day.
Nothing seemed to be out of place.
I walked into the front door of her condo in
lockstep with my mother.
Taking off my jacket, I turned around.

My body froze.
My grandfather was sitting on the sofa,
Staring directly at me.

My mother had said absolutely nothing about
him being here.
And why was he here?
My grandparents had divorced a few years after
I disclosed.

I slowly made my way up the steps,
Catching a glimpse of my grandmother in the
kitchen.
She looked back at me, and I looked at her.

No way, I protested to myself.
There is no way she's in on this too.

I stopped on the wood floor before the carpet.
My mother was acting as if nothing was out of
the ordinary.
I kept my eyes on my grandmother,

Betrayal piercing through my bones.

"Go ahead and hug your grandfather. Say hello,"
she demanded of me,
Her voice stern, forceful.

I paused; everything went fuzzy around me.
My vision returned moments later.
I stepped toward my grandfather and did as I
was told.
I hugged him, feeling my heart shatter into a
million pieces.

I wondered, *If it happens again here, are they
going to watch?*

Standing among the three of them,
My body felt dead inside, trapped,
Like a bird with its wings clipped, locked in a
cage.

"One day you will be able to fly," I whispered to
myself.
"One day you will indeed be able to fly."

Dance with Me

In junior high, I made out with two of my close girlfriends during a sleepover.
The next morning, my mother, standing in the kitchen, asked me why we had stayed up so late.

I frankly shared, "We were telling jokes and making out."

Her expression shifted; disgust arrived on her face.
She scoffed at me, making her usual remark about how I wasn't supportive of her sexuality.
I attempted to remind her that it wasn't her sexuality I had a problem with.
It was her lack of mothering, her alcoholism, and her choosing partners who encouraged this behavior that I had a problem with.

She sipped her coffee as she started to turn away from me and walk down the stairs.

I was furious at myself for stepping back into this dance with her.
She loved this dance.

I thought, *She loves this dance more than she loves me.*

Strings

I was sixteen,
Sitting in the waiting room of my primary care
doctor's office.
My mother was sitting next to me.
I went back and forth for many minutes,
wondering If I was going to tell her I wanted to
go into the appointment alone.

I felt pressure.
My stomach hurt.
My throat was closing.
We always did doctor's visits together.
She told me when I was little that her doctor
had sexually abused her and that it wasn't safe
to be in the doctor's room alone.

I said, "I think I'm going to go in alone this time."
My mother looked over at me with deep concern.
She started to panic,
But this time,
I didn't allow her to influence me.

I didn't change my mind.

Sitting on the exam table, I could hardly move.
My body was completely frozen.
I didn't want to speak or answer the doctor's questions.
I was scanning everything, prepared for the worst.

Nothing out of the ordinary happened.
I wondered, *Am I still supposed to be afraid?*

Blood on the Concrete

"Taylor!" I heard my sister scream from a distance.
I raced out of bed and ran downstairs,

My heart pounding, my belly aching, and my legs tingling.
"Just get there," I whispered to myself.
Landing on the last step, I glanced out the back slider.

My mother was face down on the concrete.
It was half past six in the morning.
She had been there all night.

A pool of blood surrounding her,
And an empty plastic green cup beside her.
I ran to her side and knelt down.

The smell of alcohol pierced my senses.

I gently rolled her body to see the damage.
Her face was gashed, full of blood.

She hissed at me,
Her words hardly recognizable.

My heart sank.

She ended up on the couch.
I looked to my sister for support.
"I can't stay here; I have to go to work," she argued.
So do I, I thought.

Why am I always the one cleaning up her messes?

I looked back at her: face torn,
Dried blood,
New blood smeared all over.

I tried to comfort her.

I was dying inside,
Dreaming of the day when this would all end.

Dark Eyes

There were beer cans everywhere and
A woman sleeping on the couch.
My mother strolled into the hallway.

A man brushed past me and stepped out the
door.
I screamed at him as he left,
Surprised by my own expression.

My mother started in on me,
Belligerent,
Furious I had ruined her night.
"Who are these people!?" I screamed at her.

Her spirit was gone, her eyes dark.
I knew this version of her all too well.

"If you don't like it here, go live with your father!
Oh wait, he never wanted you either!" she
slurred out.

I sucked in a breath; I could feel tears coming.
I could handle picking her up off the floor and
tucking her in at night.

I could handle the hypervigilance and the managing.

But I knew I was overpowered when I saw her eyes dark like this.
She knew how bad that statement stung.

I had spent my whole life trying to get my father to love me.
I wrote letters and excelled in school and sports.

Nothing.

I turned to walk away, wondering who was going to pick up all those beer cans.

Dead Dogs

I was driving home on the highway.
It was pitch-black.
I had already missed curfew by fifteen minutes.

I was seventeen.

I pulled onto the exit ramp,
Where my eyes caught a quick flash of a black
and white dog,
And then felt a

Crash.

Once off the ramp, I stopped.
Full of panic,
I started to cry.

"Why?!" I called out. Why did it have to be
a dog?!
"Please make sure he went fast and that he is
safely in doggy heaven," I pleaded.
I drove home.

"You have to ask her," I told myself.
"I can't. She will know I'm late.

"But the dog!" I exclaimed.

I went downstairs to my mother's room.
She was half asleep.

My whole body started to shake.
My voice could barely get words out.
"I hit a dog," I said.
"What do I do?
Call the police?
Call the Humane Society?

"I need help."

My body started to make noises.

Why?! I thought. *Just hold it all in.*
I had to pee; my heart was racing;
Tears were slowly falling from my eyes.

My vagina made a noise from all my body
tension.

My mother rolled over and looked at me.
"You are disgusting." She laughed and rolled
over to go back to sleep.

Humiliated, I walked back up the stairs,
Praying someone would bury that dog.

Hospital Floors

It was Mother's Day.
I was sitting on the floor in a room in the intensive
care unit at the University of Michigan—
My mother's hospital room.
She was intubated, her belly was distended,
and she had jaundice.

The physician told us she had about a year left
of her life.

She was dying.

I knew this,
But hearing it from someone else's vocal cords
hit me differently.
The drive to the hospital was long.
I was staring at the floor and the medical
equipment in the room.
Several hours passed.
I stepped out of my mother's room for a change
of scenery.

"Happy Mother's Day," I whispered to her.

Open Wounds

I walked in the front door and immediately
noticed the burn on her head.
It was an open wound the size of my fist.
We locked eyes, standing next to each other.

I could hardly breathe.

She asked me to help her, and I empathetically
agreed.
I knew she had been waiting for me to arrive to
make this request of me.

My stomach turned.

I grabbed the hydrogen peroxide as she leaned
over the sink.
Her wound fizzed as she winced with pain.
I was holding back my tears.

I quietly asked what happened.

She said she fell into the fireplace.
I sucked in a breath,
Knowing we were nearing the end of this road.

I forced a half smile and started cleaning up the sink.
She walked out of the bathroom.

Inside I was grieving.
I always had been,
But this time it felt different.

I stood there a moment longer, staring at myself in the mirror.

I didn't recognize myself.
Where are you? I wondered

I finished cleaning up the counter and hit the light switch as I closed the door behind me.

Gurneys in the Garage

I noticed that the silence was longer than usual.
I was always aware of her whereabouts.
I stepped into the garage.

Her body was lying on the concrete.
She had fallen from the white bench and was
Foaming at the mouth with her eyes rolled back
into her head.

My body was trembling feeling full panic.

I ran to grab my phone and dialed 911.
This was a familiar routine.

My whole body still shook.
My voice constricted from holding back my
emotions.

The gurney arrived.
Her BAC was 0.00, but the EMT
Still questioned her drinking.
She's detoxing. You obviously don't get it, I
thought.
Get her to the hospital.

I looked at her dead in the eyes before they wheeled her off.
Her eyes were soft, childlike, afraid.

Knowing flooded my being for a snapshot,
Her little self flashing before my eyes,
The image leaving as quickly as it had arrived.

Her expression was genuine.
"I'm sorry," she mouthed as I watched the gurney leave.

My whole body wanted to crumble and fall down.
Keep it together. Don't feel just yet, I said to myself.
I nodded and gave her a reassuring look.

I watched the ambulance doors close and the vehicle drive off.
I collapsed on the garage steps, my head in my hands.

Like an open wound repeatedly being punctured.

I held myself, leaning against the wood cabinet.
Class was starting soon,

And I still had to make it all the way downtown.
Dreading my existence,
I quickly gathered my book bag,
Wiped my face, and closed the garage door
behind me.

Every Ending Brings a New Beginning

The morning of my community college graduation ceremony,
My mother was admitted to hospice.
I spent the morning at the hospital sitting with the final decision, noticing
The gray carpet, the white walls, and the medical staff with pamphlets and clipboards.

I walked into my mother's hospital room to communicate that I would be leaving for my ceremony prior to her transfer.
My throat burned as I held back my emotions.

She told me to send her photos of myself in my cap and gown.
I silently nodded, and as I hugged her goodbye, she said,

"Stand up straight, hold your head high, and be proud of yourself, Taylor."

In the five years that followed,
I walked across two more stages,

Receiving my bachelor's degree in psychology
And my master's degree in clinical social work.

As a first-generation college graduate
And the first person in my family to hold a
graduate degree,

I loved to learn.
I still do.

My curiosity about people, systems, cultures,
and the world around me made the classroom
one of my most favorite places to be.

The words "I promise to always leave room for
learning, unlearning, and relearning" are written
with black Sharpie on my bathroom mirror,

A daily reminder for the critical parent voice
inside my head to give the little girl inside me a
break once in a while.

Is This an Episode of *Jerry Springer*?

My grandmother tasked my sister and me with picking out my mother's funeral outfit after she died.
A part of me wanted to put her in something absolutely ridiculous.

She had a sweatshirt that read, "I'm what Willis was talking about."

I resisted the urge and chose a simple long-sleeve purple top,
Her favorite color.
My sister and I were gathering the clothes in her closet to donate.
My mother's girlfriend at the time and her cousin were upstairs in the living room.

Moments later, I found myself standing in the kitchen
Next to my sister,
Facing the two of them across the kitchen island.

My sister had words to exchange after my mother's girlfriend was declaring the home was hers.

The cousin started in, stepping toward my sister. My sister was about to have her teeth knocked in by this forty-something-year-old woman who looked as if she was ready for the up-close camera shot on *Jerry Springer.*

This wasn't her first rodeo.

Instinct taking over,
I stepped in front of my sister, who stepped directly behind me.
"Stop, you guys! I exclaimed,
Tears streaming down my face, my body shivering.

I looked directly at my mother's girlfriend.

"Seriously, Mom would not have wanted any of this," I said,
Still looking her straight in the eyes.
They backed off, eventually leaving altogether.

For years I choked on this moment,
Angry with myself that after all this time,

I still wanted to protect my sister.
And my mother.
It was messed up, and it also made absolute
sense.

I stepped outside to catch my breath.
Putting my hair in a ponytail, I looked up to the
sky and thought,

*My mother is seriously the gift that keeps on
giving.*

A Note Taped on My Mother's Door

I was a senior in high school when I stumbled upon Elizabeth Gilbert's work.
A quote from *Eat Pray Love* reads,
"Look for God. Look for God like a man with his head on fire looks for water."
I wrote this quote down on a piece of 3" × 5" lined yellow paper notepad that my mother kept in the junk drawer in the kitchen.

I taped it on the outside of her bedroom door for her.

It never moved until the day I took it down after she passed away.
I tucked it inside of the box in which I kept some of the notes she had written me over the years.

She asked me one day if I had put it there.
I nodded, and she smiled.

We never had a conversation about it, but maybe we didn't have to.
Maybe there were some things that didn't need explaining at all.

The Best Way I Know How

John Steinbeck wrote, "Try to understand men. If you understand each other, you will be kind to each other. Knowing a man well never leads to hate and almost always leads to love."

I spoke these words standing in front of a crowded room at my mother's funeral.

There weren't enough seats in the room to hold all the people.
Some were even standing along the back wall,
Filling in any empty standing space that was left.

Prior to my speech, the pastor had my grandmother, me, and my sister stand up and turn around to witness how many people filled the room.

I spoke about the home videos, her recording my sister and me when we were little.
I shared stories of the dance recitals, the softball games, and the summers riding Jet Skis.

I also named the elephant in the room, the alcoholism, her pain—
The reason I was standing at the podium speaking to begin with.

At the end of my speech,
I invited everyone to stand and dance to a song by one of my mother's favorite singers, Lady Gaga, "Born This Way."

The music started to play over the speakers,
And I asked the director of the funeral home to turn the volume up a little more.

It was the best way I knew how to celebrate my mother's spirit,

Surrounded by the people whose lives she had touched along the way,
And with parting words from Lady Gaga:
"Rejoice and love yourself today because, baby, you were born this way."

Death

My grandmother was admitted to hospice a couple of years after my mother passed away.
If you had asked her,
She would have told you she died from a broken heart.

She would have no hesitation in admitting that
My mother was her everything.

At the time, I was working full time in refugee foster care,
Attending night classes for a master's degree,
And squeezing my clinical internship hours into the little remaining time I had left in the day.

I was also visiting my grandmother every day.
The pressure felt insurmountable.

I decided to take two days off from visiting my grandmother.
The next time I saw her,
She was angry with me,
Inquiring why I hadn't come to see her.

I closed my eyes and took a deep breath.

My mother's face popped into my head.
Empathy and compassion washed over my body in that moment as I
Understood the weight of expectation she also must have felt, even as a little girl.

My grandmother was the youngest of four girls,
Raised mostly by her older sisters.
Her mother, Caroline, was a single mother.

My grandmother changed her original burial plans.
Instead of being placed next to my grandfather,
She would be cremated and her ashes placed in the columbarium with my mother's ashes.

I thought it was an interesting choice to make,
But I kept my comments to myself.

One evening, we sat on the edge of her hospice bed together.
I thanked her for helping to support my mother and to raise my sister and me.

Tears filled her eyes, and she softly said, "Taylor, I may have done you more harm than I have good all these years. Promise me you will continue to always be all that you can be."

I silently nodded and gave her a hug before saying good night.

My grandmother passed away within one month of her cancer diagnosis on my sister's birthday. I wasn't sure if this was another passive-aggressive message or just a very odd coincidence.

Part II

Mirrors

I'm a Goddess on My Knees

(Lyrics by: Meredith Brooks
Song Title: Bitch)

I started reading *Cosmopolitan* magazine when
I was twelve.
The issues belonged to my sister, who was
fifteen at the time.
I used to sneak them out of her room and read
them in my own when no one was watching,

Listening to Meredith Brooks, Alanis Morissette,
Madonna, and Taylor Dayne.

I learned all about the perfect blow job,
How to make him want me, and
All the things I needed to know to be desirable.

What I wasn't aware of was that the magazine
was never going to tell me I had low self-esteem
and low self-worth
And that instead of searching for it outside
myself,

I might want to try searching within myself.

That awareness didn't transcend into my consciousness until I was twenty-six, asking my partner at the time for a divorce.

I started putting all my *Cosmopolitan* knowledge into practice when I was in junior high school.

The guy I was infatuated with also happened to be the guy from whom, later, our high school bought water bottles full of vodka.

He was a businessman,
An entrepreneur let's say.
When I was thirteen, he was my boyfriend.

He also liked to hook up with his sister's friend when I wasn't around.
It made for an interesting story.

In the years that followed, similar experiences presented themselves with not so glamorous endings.

Cosmopolitan had officially failed me.

The Magical Forest

During recess in second grade,
I made nature crowns with my friends while sitting under the trees.
I would weave tree leaves together with pine needles,
Stitching them together to make a crown.

Once I returned from recess,
My teacher did not allow my nature crown to be worn in her room.

I wanted to inform her I was a goddamn fairy queen.

Alas, I did as I was told.
She did, however, allow her son to visit the classroom to play his guitar.

This creativity was celebrated.

As a class, we were instructed to pick up five things off the floor to help keep the room tidy.
This behavior received a large amount of praise.

Most days, I enjoyed this activity,
Turning it into a scavenger hunt for little treasures.

That day, I picked up three things
As an act of sheer rebellion,
My seven-year-old self protesting,
There is room for my nature crown too, dammit.

I'm Just Here, Trying to Be a Spice Girl

In every photo of me from kindergarten to third grade, I am posing with the peace sign, referencing girl power and my favorite all-girl band, the Spice Girls.
The platform shoes, the minidresses, the microphones, and the friends who were like sisters.

Everything I had ever wanted.

Once I started dressing myself,
I chose clothes that completely covered my body.
For many years, I wore only athletic clothes,
Feeling more comfortable when my body was hidden.
Even when I wasn't physically being invaded,
Throughout my life,
People seemed to comment on my body a lot,

My grandmother telling me I needed to wear more makeup,
My mother telling me I didn't need it,

A softball coach telling me I had nice thighs,
But adding that if I toned them,
They would look even better,
A girlfriend pointing out the red bumps on my thighs when it was warm out,
And a coworker commenting that an outfit wouldn't work for me because I didn't have any hips.

Inside, I felt defeated.

All I wanted was to be in my all-girl band,
Wearing a minidress with platform boots and singing my heart out,

Surrounded by people who were filled with love.

Queen of Wands

Mrs. Stephens was my fourth-grade teacher
And was one of the coolest people I have ever
known.
She would play music and have us stand at our
desks and dance for a few minutes on Fridays.
She would stand at her desk and dance too.
I learned all about the shopping cart, the
sprinkler, and the lawn mower from Mrs.
Stephens.

Whenever she would tell us it was time to stand
and dance,
I was terrified.
My body wanted to immediately hide or excuse
myself and beeline it to the bathroom.

But my heart?
She was ecstatic, wondering,
Does Mrs. Stephens know how much I love to
dance?
I love being free, feeling the music, and moving
my body!
And then came the fear.

Don't move. Don't let anyone see you. It's not safe.

I was very conflicted.
Mrs. Stephens would also lead story time.
She read us "Peppermints in the Parlor."
We would gather around her chair,
Sitting on the floor in the front of the classroom.
I was in awe of Mrs. Stephens.
She would embody the characters, using different voices and sounds.

Mrs. Stephens was larger than life.

One reading time in particular, Mrs. Stephens informed us it was perfectly OK to pass gas if we had to.
She said that if we didn't let the gas out of our bodies,
It would cause our digestive systems to back up.
Then she made direct eye contact with me.
I pretended she hadn't while still holding in my fart.

She continued reading.

My eyes glued on Mrs. Stephens, I wondered,
Does Mrs. Stephens know I love performing too!?"
I would lose myself in the story, using my
imagination to color in a whole new world.
I looked forward to story time in her classroom
each day.

Imagination was my safe place,
A place to dream and feel,
A place to create a world that was filled with
love, belonging,
And sparkles—lots and lots of gold sparkles.

The Freedom to Choose

Mrs. Stephens told me one day that I would be receiving additional assignments in her class to work on when I was finished with my other classwork.
She asked if I would be OK with doing extra assignments.
"Yes," I said to her.
Inside, I was very excited to choose my own assignments and learn more about something I was interested in.

I chose to complete a presentation on Hawaii.

Mrs. Stephens allowed me to visit the library,
My most favorite place,
And research Hawaii during class time.

I felt so free.

Once my presentation was complete,
Mrs. Stephens asked what classroom I wanted to present my work to.
My eyes lit up. Immediately Mrs. Hubbard came to mind.

Mrs. Hubbard was my first-grade teacher.
She was warm and cozy, and she gave the best hugs.

I felt safe with Mrs. Hubbard.

I ran down to her classroom to ask permission to present in her room.
She agreed!
I presented my poster and my information on Hawaii to Mrs. Hubbard's students while I was sitting in her reading chair.

I was very nervous and excited.

Mrs. Hubbard assisted me along the way with the names of the islands.
Her students gathered around me, listening intently.
When I was finished,
Mrs. Hubbard gave me a hug, and her students thanked me.
I skipped down the hallway back to Mrs. Stephens's room,
Hoping the library volunteers were busy
So I could skip the whole rest of the way.

Sex and Duct Tape: It's a Onetime-Only Deal

In junior high, I was enrolled in a Life Transitions class.

It was the class where you learn about meth, friendships, and sex.

This specific day was a class activity day,

My least favorite of days.

My teacher was standing in front of the classroom with a roll of duct tape.

She said that engaging in sexual behavior with multiple people is like reusing the same piece of duct tape to hold something in place.

If you use it more than once, it starts to lose its connection.

She then proceeded to hand a piece of duct tape to each student in the room.

We were instructed to go around and touch the same corner piece to multiple other individuals' corner pieces and notice how the tape lost its stickiness with the more pieces it touched.

I questioned to myself:

So, if I engage in sexual behavior with one partner and we don't work out, that means I won't have as good of a connection with the next person?
And if this is the case, then that second person and I definitely wouldn't work out, so I should probably just stay with the first person?
But what if I don't like that first person anymore?
That seems like a lot of pressure to get it right on the first go-round.

This feels like a trick.
I looked at my teacher and down at my piece of duct tape.

More questions.

But what if your first sexual experience was when you were really, really little?
Teeny-tiny?
My whole body cringed.
Am I doomed forever because of this?!

Maybe raise your hand and ask her, I thought.
This was followed by,

Absolutely not.
Definitely do not raise your hand and ask that question.

This duct tape information is definitely false, I decided.

More questions.

Who is paying this woman to teach me false information?
The government?
Taxpayers?
My mother popped into my head.
Oh no, I thought.
My mother is going to be very upset to know her taxes from working hard as a single mother are paying for this woman's salary to teach me false information.

I giggled to myself, still holding the piece of duct tape.

Ace of Wands

Next period, I found myself sifting through magazines for a project.
We were learning about science, nature, and writing.
A lightbulb went off in my brain.
That's it! That's what I want to do!

I want to write and take photos for National Geographic.
I can spend time in nature, be with the animals, write, and take photos!
That will be the perfect job for me! I exclaimed to myself.

I raised my hand.

"How does someone write and take photos for *National Geographic*?" I asked.
My teacher appeared a bit peeved by my question and went on to explain that one doesn't just start working for *National Geographic*.
She said people start their writing careers working for journals or a small local magazine, but that oftentimes they have another job

supporting them because it's hard to earn a living entirely by writing.

My heart sank.

"But what if I don't want to work for a local journal?" I said to myself quietly.

Dream killer, another part of me replied inside my head.

This also sounds a bit subjective, I thought.

"Oh, OK, thank you," I said politely.

First the duct tape, now this?! I thought.
Who is in charge of all this?!

Rock Star Status

On the first day of my eighth-grade English class,
The following statement was written on the whiteboard.
"When I grow up, I want to be _____."
After the bell rang, my teacher stood in front of the class and said,
"Hello, everyone. My name is Mrs. Kooi, and when I grow up, I want to be a rock star."

I started laughing out loud.
Sold, immediately, I thought.
This woman needs to be president of the United States.

Maybe Mrs. Kooi would want to be in my all-girl band? I thought.
Definitely don't ask her today, but maybe another time.

Packing up my books to head to next period,
I knew eighth-grade English was going to be one of my most favorite classes of the entire year.

Sixteen

Your blue Chevy.
My bare feet on the dash.
You always reached for my hand first.

I wore your jersey in the halls
Those two years.
I held out.
Your hand holding mine,

Playing ball together,
Drinking tea with your mom on the back porch—
You were one of my best friends.

Mom was getting bad again.
That summer, your parents split,
Both our hearts aching.

On the kitchen counter
In your mom's new place,
Your head moved down my bare pelvis

My hand covered my mouth, giggling.
You started laughing too.

That night we won both our games.
You leaned over and whispered,
"Tay, I'm in love with you."

My Opening Act

At the start of my senior year of high school,
I landed myself a stay in the intensive care unit.
During my hospitalization, the physician communicated with me they were concerned I might have leukemia or lymphoma—cancer.
The next morning, I was prepped for the procedure.

My nurse informed me I would be receiving medication for my fever through my butt.

Once I was ready, she wheeled me down to the procedure room.
They positioned me on the table.
As the anesthesiologist began to explain the medicine I would be receiving through my IV,
I caught a glimpse of my mother standing in the doorway, sobbing.
The medical team was informing her she needed to step out of the room.
She was refusing to leave.

I wished, *Someone please handle this. I physically cannot move.*

Several staff members assisted my mother out the door, and I watched the white liquid enter my IV.

Once I was back in my hospital room, my grandmother asked if I remembered anything when I woke up from the procedure.

I shook my head no.

She replied, "Well, you told the entire medical team you had a rocket ship put up your ass this morning.

Apparently, you had the room in tears with your jokes."

It hurt to giggle, my body was in so much pain.

Relief washed over my insides as I thought,
I am still in there!
Maybe I'm not dead after all.
Maybe I've just been hiding.

Judgment

In college, I was introduced to a church in west Michigan.
I applied to be a youth group leader after attending Sunday services.
As I entered a small office,
Résumé in hand,
I met with a woman who appeared to be in her mid-twenties.
The position was leading a small group circle for fifth- and sixth- or seventh- and eighth-grade students.

She asked me during the interview if I had ever been a victim or perpetrator of physical, sexual, or emotional abuse.
I wondered,
What does this have to do with my ability to lead a small group for one hour once a week? Does she really want me to elaborate on all this?
I answered her question truthfully,
And her demeanor immediately shifted.

She asked me to clarify if I was the perpetrator or the victim.

My throat started to close; I could feel the tears behind my eyes.
"Victim," I heard myself say,
My body constricting, feeling defeated, exposed.
I hated that word.
I wanted nothing to do with that word.

She clarified that the purpose for the introductory questions was to ensure the safety of the group members.
I started to feel really small,
Questioning whether I was currently safe being in the interview.
The following questions were about my sexual activity in my current relationship.

The woman asked me if I was engaging in premarital sex.

"Yes," I answered her.
This time, her demeanor completely changed.

The interview ended shortly after that, and I drove home
Feeling like a crumb.

I received an email later from the woman stating I had not been chosen for the position.
In the email, she cited that my decision to engage in premarital sex was a reason for my not being selected.

My whole body filled with sensations as I read her message.
I wondered, *Does everyone in this church hold this belief?*
And if they do, are they practicing what they preach?

I didn't share in this belief.
To the contrary,
I felt it was a harmful message.
My attendance at services dwindled after this experience.

A year later, while working as a psychiatric technician,
I received another email asking if I would be interested in the youth group leader position.

My eyes locked on the computer screen for several moments as I

Recalled the interview and the woman's previous email.
I had so many words to say.

I chose to close my laptop instead.
Several thoughts popped into my head.

Maybe I should reply that I'm still bumpin' and grindin' without a ring on my left ring finger symbolizing it is acceptable to do so.
Do I send Pretty Ricky song lyrics?
Definitely don't share that my mother is a lesbian.
I laughed to myself while also repulsed by the fact that this woman held a position in leadership.

How many other women have had a similar experience? I wondered.

Leaving the nurses' station to visit with the next patient on my list,
I made it a point to show up with even more kindness and empathy.

It was the best way I knew of to offer balance to this world.

Knight of Pentacles

I caught your stare the minute I walked through
the door.
I was studying psychology.

You were studying me.

A country bar in the city.
You asked me to dance.

"Neon Moon."

Something told me it was OK to trust you.
You led, and I followed.

You kept a black-and-white photo of me on your
nightstand.
I spent weeknights watching you play.
When I couldn't sleep,
You always answered,

"Door's open. Come crawl in next to me."

Your Beach Street rental turned into a Cape
Cod home for two.
I asked your mom for recipes.

We painted the kitchen neutral.
That spring was the halo engagement ring.

Summer came, and I boarded a plane.

The cobblestones called.
I was studying Roman architecture and history.
You wanted the small town.

I wanted to run wild in the streets of Capri.

You have a family of your own now
In that same small town.

I'm still sitting by the sea.
I wonder at times
If your heart still thinks of me.

The Tower

I was in my early twenties when someone noticed.
A sexual partner at the time stopped midintercourse and said,

"You aren't even here with me right now."

That was the first time anyone was in tune with my lack of presence.

There I was
Lying on his mattress
That lay directly on his bedroom floor.

Romantic.

I had been called out.
But he was right:

I wasn't present.

Recalling my past experiences,
I could tell all the details.
The feelings, sensations.

Was it just this one time?
Or were there others?

I wondered.
He asked me to try something.

He asked me to hold his gaze while we had sex.
I was on bottom.
Feeling extremely unsure, I agreed.

We proceeded.

I held his gaze and thought I had passed the test.
He paused and said, "Right there, I just lost you again."

Fuck, he was right.

I couldn't even see his face at that point,
And he was literally on top of me.
This new awareness hit me like a ton of bricks.

I didn't know whether to laugh or cry,
A repetitive theme in my life circling its way around again.
The universe is funny like that though.

I Wonder if She Knew

I was twenty-two years old.
During the day, I was working as a foster care
case manager.
At night, I was attending graduate classes for a
master's degree in clinical social work.
I received the call.
It was the end of the day,
And I knew I had to go get her.
She was fifteen, a permanent court ward, and
desperately wanted to remain in her familial
placement.

She was in a hotel just off the highway exit.

I chose to go without police and agency support.
Something told me this would only be successful
if I went alone.

I pulled in, knowing this removal would change
her entire life.

She was going to live with a tribal member,
The next best option to kin—
If best option was even an option in this scenario.

I knocked on the hotel room door.
When she saw it was me, her face dropped.

She knew.

I sat on the hotel bed for a while,
Talking with her, her family, and her friend from school.

I was transparent.

She would be leaving with me and placed in a new town,
More than an hour away, at a new school, knowing absolutely no one.

After some time passed and numerous negotiations,
She walked out with me.

I observed from a distance as she hugged her family goodbye,
Tears streaming down her face.
Once she climbed in my passenger seat,
She began expressing her anger.
I was quiet, allowing room for her expression.

The only statement I offered during the car ride was,

"If you're going to punch me, I need a heads-up to pull over. It's too dangerous on the highway." I said frankly.

"Fair," she said back with a half-smile, resting her head on the window.

I received recognition for my work from the higher-ups at the agencies involved in this case. It was rewarding to have my work acknowledged, But my heart still had an unfulfilled desire.

As I spent time with these children and their families day in and day out,
I noticed how generations of pain was perpetuated,
Cycles repeating in the next generation.

The system was failing these cases.

There was a lack of funding, lack of community supports, even lack of caseworkers.

I noticed how the general population was unaware of these children and their families suffering,
Going about their day-to-day lives, sitting in traffic with their coffees,
Oblivious that there are children desperately needing tomorrow to be different from today.

I wondered,

What would need to change within the system or the culture to provide better outcomes for these children?

I kept the flowers I received from the agency as recognition for mediating this case.
It's been almost ten years.

One remaining flower sits dried in the small vase on my kitchen sink.
I leave it out as a reminder of that day and of her,
And I hope that somehow, she knows I still think of her.

She, too, held her mother's pain.
I wonder if she knew.

I had spent the past decade in the field of social work,
Serving vulnerable populations in the settings of addiction,
Foster care,
Refugee services, and
Medical social work,
Eventually transitioning into private practice.

I had witnessed case after case,
Family after family,
Suffering for the exact same reason.

Pain was being passed generationally and expressed in numerous ways.

A mother addicted to prescription benzodiazepines to numb the pain of her relationship with her partner.
A medically fragile five-year-old girl being adopted by her grandparents, who was born into this world through incest, creating a life-limiting disease.
Teenage refugees fleeing their home countries because of gang violence and war, losing their families and homes.

A twenty-one-year-old female in the emergency
room who attempted suicide by hanging herself
from a tree in a forest each year on her birthday.

Witnessing those moments,
Evaluating those patients,
Holding space for those families,
Testifying in courtrooms,
Mediating next-of-kin medical decision-making—
Whichever role I took that day,

I noticed

Story after story,
The weaving of the web.
It was all connected.

We were all connected.

Express Yourself

Title by: Madonna

I was back in Judy's office after my mother died.
In one of our sessions,
Judy shared with me that my mother,
Before she passed away,
Had asked her to look after me.

Judy was a woman ahead of her time.
She trained in EMDR in the 1990s,
Was a sex therapist,
And quoted Gloria Steinem frequently.
She always told me I would be a therapist
one day.
At the time, I thought she was just being nice.

The joke remains always on me.

She ended every session by saying,
"Tay, it's an absolute honor every time I get to
see you. I love you,"
And offering me a giant hug as I left her office.

Judy's presence made me believe I was going
to be OK.

She believed in me when I didn't believe in myself.

During the years when I spent time in Judy's office,
She gave me a poem by Portia Nelson
Titled "Autobiography in Five Short Chapters."

It reads:

I

I walk down the street.
There is a deep hole in the sidewalk.
I fall in. I am lost. … I am hopeless.
It isn't my fault.
It takes forever to find a way out.

II

I walk down the same street.
There is a deep hole in the sidewalk.
I pretend I don't see it.
I fall in again.
I can't believe I'm in the same place.
But it isn't my fault.
It still takes a long time to get out

III
I walk down the same street.
There is a deep hole in the sidewalk.
I see it is there.
I still fall in. It's a habit.
My eyes are open.
I know where I am.
It is my fault.
I get out immediately.

IV

I walk down the same street.
There is a deep hole in the sidewalk.
I walk around it.

V

I walk down another street.

I Walked Down the Same Street

It all fell apart.
We broke it.
Put together with string, Band-Aids, and glitter
glue.
I blew the final whistle.

These are the facts.

There we were building a life together day
after day.
I would watch him sometimes doing yard work
outside.
I would wonder,
*Is this what everyone was rushing down the
aisle for?*

Was this the life he wanted for himself?
Why am I even here?

It seemed as if we were two people who did
what we thought we were supposed to be doing
based on societal conditioning,
Physical attraction,

And apparently a deep sense of loneliness that we both called love.

I was thinking more about attraction these days and how sometimes attraction can feel like quicksand,
Where at first you're on this adrenaline ride that feels so intense, You're basically high.
But by the time you come back to reality,
You realize you are very much in the middle of the sand,
Sinking along with your self-respect.

But love.
How do we define love?

That felt bigger, a higher, more elevated way of being.
A lighter, softer sinking,
Which actually turns out not to sink you at all,
But set you free.

Tell It to My Heart
Song Title by Taylor Dayne

I didn't see it coming.

I was in the sun, out on the water, with a group
of friends,
Happily drifting away with the waves.
The water always made my life better somehow.

He kneeled down in front of me and looked me
dead in the eyes.

This life-changing moment happened to be
about a sandwich and what I wanted to eat for
lunch.
He asked me what I wanted in a way that told
me he would give me the moon and the stars
and hand-deliver them to me that very day.

Time stood still.

It was a feeling I had never known before.
So foreign.
I was wondering what the hell was happening
inside my chest.

He was always telling me I needed to learn how to let people in.

I usually followed this statement up with an eye roll.

I was just now putting together that what he was really saying

Was to let him in.

It was the first time my entire body wanted to melt into another human being's.

I felt safe in his presence, secure.
He was centimeters from me, our bodies almost touching.

I broke his eye contact and looked behind him,
Catching the direct glare of the woman he had brought with him.
The boat stopped at the dock.
I excused myself to the restroom.
The woman he had brought with him followed behind me.
As I was washing my hands in the restroom, she approached me.

"So, you guys have always been just friends?" she questioned me.

"Yeah, just friends," I casually said, washing my hands.

I gave a quick smile and turned to walk out the door.

Before leaving, I caught her eyes staring at me in the bathroom mirror.

"Mm-hmm," I heard her hum as I walked out the door.

You Can't Blame Brené Brown

We were sitting in the three-season room,
Discussing the terms of our separation.
"You know you're divorcing me because you
started reading Brené Brown," he jokingly said.
I laughed out loud, thinking, *False.*

I offered to lend him one of Brené's books I had.
I had spent months asking him to read one of
her books.
This time, he kindly accepted,
And I downloaded one of her audiobooks onto
his phone.

A few months later, we sat together in the living
room reviewing the divorce paperwork over
Chinese takeout.
I completed the terms and the paperwork I had
received at the courthouse.
He reviewed them, and we both signed on the
dotted line.

No lawyers,
No courtrooms,
Just the two of us
And a box of Chinese takeout.

Isn't It Ironic? Don't You think?
Song Lyrics from Alanis Morsette song Ironic

Red rocks, the earth beneath my bones.
Four days, only four days in the desert.
I felt a ping in my pelvis.
Excusing myself to the restroom.
Wet underwear.
Clear, stringy juice.
My juice.
I'm ovulating!
It had been more than a hundred days.
I was two thousand miles away from the person
I was trying to ovulate near.
We had tried for months, but my body was refusing.
Here?
Now?
The irony made me nauseous.

The voice: *You know this isn't what you want for her.*
I placed a hand on my heart, my mind finally joining.

I signed on the dotted line.

This time around, my insides were bursting with joy.

Paperwork filed.

It no longer whispered from the back of my dresser drawer, shoved under my sweaters.

The unknown. I was ready.

The High Priestess

I was sitting on my bathroom floor,
The one we had remodeled together the year prior.
She said to me firmly,
"Taylor, the process is the outcome."
Woof, I thought. *What a long process.*

She assigned meditation as my homework.
Three minutes, timed, sitting still, observing my thoughts.
I also joined a local yoga studio for hot yoga classes.

I fell in love with yin hot yoga.

Slipping off my shoes in the entryway before class,
I heard a staff member cheerfully say to another guest arriving,
"Hi, John. It's nice to see you."
The man kindly replied,

"Wow, it is so nice to be seen."

The Tin Man

The minute I heard your voice,
I knew.
The moment you first saw me,
I felt you,
An instant remembering,
Your unexplainable force
Magnetized itself beside me.

Without an invitation,

I'd watch you from afar,
Amused by your posturing.
You chose an interesting costume.

This time around,

Your heart wasn't in medicine.
This was clear as day.
I wondered how you strayed so far
And what happened along the way.

I wanted to reach for your hand
So you would remember me too.
Something told me we would be dancing apart

Until the time turned blue.

Treasures in the Desert

I was guided to visit the red rocks again to have
a reading.
As a woman who loves a good quest, I accepted.
I met a woman who shared the same name as
my mother.
She said, "I don't normally do this, but I'd like to
read for you if you're open to it."

I smiled.
"I would love that. Thank you," I replied.

We sat together at her kitchen table.
She said, "There's a very strong feminine energy
coming in. She's a Pisces."
Knowing flooded my body. "It's my mom" I said
softly, chills filling my body.
My mother, a Pisces sun, Scorpio moon, and
Cancer rising.
"She's here with you right now. Are you moving?
She's supporting this move for you big-time."
I smiled, tears filling my eyes.
"She's saying you have been waiting for an
opportunity like this for a long time."
Tears were falling down my face. "Yes," I replied,

Recalling my eighteen-year-old self's dream of attending the University of North Carolina–Wilmington to study psychology and art.

I shared with her that I had chosen to attend the local community college to save money, help my grandmother, and visit my mother at the hospital between working and attending my classes.

"She's sharing that this next chapter will be for you now. The opportunity is yours if you want to take it," she said kindly.

I covered my face with my hands, sobbing. I looked at her, sharing, "I want it, and I'm taking it! Yes!"

In five weeks' time,
I passed my clinical boards,
Sold my home,
Accepted a position at a new hospital system,
Secured an apartment within walking distance,
And drove myself and my two dogs across the country

To begin a brand-new chapter.

Part III

The Star, Temperance, and the World

The more I released what did not belong to me
in my body,
The more I recalled what did belong to me:
My creativity, power, and voice.

She feels larger than life at times,

Full of personality, wit, and humor.
I returned to my love of writing and exploring.
I returned to my love of laughing, singing, and
dancing.

Photography was the first to arrive,
Followed by poetry and exploring new places.

These moments hold precious space in my
heart,
Each one collecting pieces, remembering, and
recalling.
Learning how to receive, express, and be held
so gently
By the land, the ocean, and the seas,
By the skies, the sun, and the moon,
By the people and places I encountered along
the way,
Hands that were held, warm embraces

Eyes locking, souls meeting, and time standing still.
Strokes of a paintbrush, my body moving to the sound.

Alas, my sovereignty.

It Begins and Ends with Reparenting

It took awhile before she let me see her—
Really see her.
Most days, I was patient.
Other days, I forced.

I took it all to the trees.

At first, she told me she wanted to sit on the
couch next to me with her snacks to watch
Harry Potter.
I bought the snacks.
Then she told me she wanted to swing at the
park with her music.
I went to the park with her.
Next, she wanted to go to the theater by herself
to sit in the comfy chairs and see a new film.
I took her to the comfy chairs,
Followed by a visit to the local library to sit with
the books.
We read for hours.

Once she started to trust me,
Her emotions surfaced.
I held her in the bathtub,

On my bedroom floor,
In the front seat of my car,
You name it.

I sat with her for minutes,
Sometimes for hours,
And at other times for days.

I placed one hand on my sacral chakra
And the other on my heart chakra.
I spoke to her softly, gently, with reassurance.

"I will be right here with you until you feel safe
enough to let me see you, hear you, and know
you. As long as it takes, I will be right here."

I closed my eyes,
Took a deep breath,
And allowed whatever to arise
Be seen, felt, expressed, and validated.

I welcomed all of it.

My Bones Tell Stories

I found myself wandering
Through time and space,
The mountains and the sky.

The possibilities felt endless,
Open,
Spacious.

My heart was breathing full breaths.

Something much bigger than me was coming.
I felt it

In my bones.

An Outfit for Me, Only

A pair of high-waisted shorts and a leather crop top.
It was the first time I had chosen something different to wear from what I would have selected in the past.

If anyone tells you an outfit can't change your life,
They are absolutely 100 percent wrong.

I decided I didn't want to blend in or follow some kind of programmed choice that day.

That was the old way of doing things.
Truthfully, had it really even been a choice before?

This time it felt like my soul was choosing and not my warped conditioning, needing to conform to be loved.

Every time I see this outfit in my closet,
I smile a little inside knowing this was another step toward my freedom.

How could something that seems so small on
the outside feel so big to me on the inside?

I mean, it was just shorts and a top,
But it served as this magical symbol
For the little girl inside me who was screaming
for joy

Because she was finally starting to be heard.

I Hold Her Tenderly and Speak to Her Softly

I love you.
You are the love of my life.
You are safe.
You are powerful.
Your heart is the ocean.
Your power is the sun.
Your love will change the world.
I love you.

Archways

I noticed she was alone
She wore a turquoise bathing suit,
Playing in the sand.
I knelt down beside her.
She glanced up at me and held my gaze.

Her eyes said everything.

I noticed her sword was missing.
Pointing to the archway, I placed a hand on her
back.
She nodded as if she already knew the way.
Of course she knew, I thought.
She wasn't seeking guidance.

She was waiting patiently for me.

His Name Was Raven

Not a man, but a horse.
As much as I imagined the classic Cinderella
fairy tale coming to fruition, this wasn't that
story.
I was coming back for myself
With swords and gold glittery fairy dust,
Wearing my favorite pair of 1990s high-waisted
jeans.

I received a text message from a friend inviting
me to attend a movement class with horses.
It was quarter to eight o'clock on a Sunday
morning,
An hour before the event.
My entire insides felt like fireworks of joy
exploding in my body.

The universe was speaking, and she was
coming in hot.
I accepted the invitation.

I had loved horses ever since I was a little girl,
Pure majestical beings with healing powers
beyond the mind's understanding.

The minute I walked onto the property, I felt it.
I walked through the gate, followed the therapist's instructions, and centered myself in the middle of the covered arena.
Allowing our energies to welcome each other first,
I stood across from two black stallions,
Grounding myself in the land.
My body started releasing on her own as I welcomed their presence, tears falling from my eyes.

The movement began, and I followed my breath,
My body trembling.

The therapist guided participants to move toward the outer railing for additional support.
I grabbed the metal bar tight with my left hand,
Allowing my body to sink,
With my right hand touching the earth.
I started sobbing, my stomach shaking, mucus dripping from my nose.
Moments later I glanced to my right.
The two horses, Raven and Julien,
Were gently making their way over to me.
I stood softly, meeting their presence.

I looked Raven in the eyes.

Let this go. It's time. Let me help you, he communicated.

I pulled back. *I don't know how,* I pleaded.

His muzzle started tracing my right arm.

When he reached my wrist and hand, he started licking me.

I softened.

My solar plexus expanded, full of air,

The phrase "power is not meant to be predatory" washing over me.

I sank deeper, allowing my body full expression.

I looked back at Raven, a mustang, black with a white patch on his forehead.

His eyes met mine. *You and me, we are the same, O wild one,* his eyes said with a glimmer.

I smiled, opening my heart to him a little more.

"Thank you," I whispered back, my heart full of gratitude.

Moments later, Raven and Julien strolled several feet in front of me.

I glanced out to the field, and looking back to the arena,

I noticed Raven releasing everything that was inside him in the form of a bowel movement.

He emptied the biggest pile of horse poop I had ever seen.

My eyes opened wide; I started giggling.

In a matter of minutes, Raven had transmuted memories of pain that I had held in my body for three decades.

He was the true alchemist, and I a mere student, Grateful for his teaching that morning.

Ocean Songs

Mama whale visited
Schools of fish said hello.
The orange butterflies surround my heart,
And my soul feels at home.

The River

This morning, the sun rose on the Big Island.
Bare feet in the grass, sun gazing, big breaths.
The full moon in Virgo was stirring the ocean within me.
The River presented herself this morning from the Wild Unknown Archetype.
She whispered, "Two feet in, babe. Two feet in."

If My Bathtub Could Talk

She would tell you she held me tight
Four straight years.
She would tell you I visited her

Multiple times a day.

She would tell you I held my body
Sobbing, screaming, silence.
She would tell you I felt violated, betrayed, and
abandoned.

I was really coming home.

She would tell you I loved to sing—
Write and dance too.
She would tell you all the times I brought my
snacks

To share with my favorite soul, Stu.

The Dark Forest

I was starting to get the feeling that none of this
belonged to me.
I was lost—
And not the "lost and eventually being found"
kind of lost.

I was in the dark woods alone, up-a-shit-creek-
without-a-paddle kind of lost.

I didn't know where to go or who to even ask.
How did I get here?
But I was here now, and I had to find a way out.

I was good at that.
Looking for the exits,
It came naturally to me,
But I didn't see an exit this time

Anywhere.

So, I sat down, taking it all in.
I was frustrated.
I hated feelings, and now I was acutely aware I
had many of them.

I preferred avoidance, distractions.
I was so good at distractions.

There was something about this place that told
me I'd have to sit here awhile
By myself with no distractions.

Painful.

I had to learn how to move with it and not
against it.
I had to learn ease.
What was ease?
How does one stumble upon ease?
That word was foreign to my vocabulary,
Let alone my central nervous system.

But here I was, learning all about ease.
Not well, to be honest.
I thrived in chaos.
Give me all the scattered energy and I could
problem-solve that shit in my sleep.

I chose a career navigating complex problems,
Which seemed a bit hilarious in this moment now.

Just because someone is good at something and it's familiar,
Does that mean it's the best choice?

Choice.
The word *choice*.
Language is highly defining,
Yet we hardly think twice about it.

My word for the year is *choice*.

My Parts Have a Sit-Down Pep Talk

You are not alone.
I am here with you.

I hate this feeling, I hate this feeling, I hate this feeling.

It is safe to let go.
Other people are not your responsibility.

I need more space, I need more space, I need more space.

This pain is only temporary.
Don't you dare give up on yourself.

I need to scream, I need to scream, I need to scream.

Allow your body to breathe.
Remember who you are.

I can follow my heart.

I Am Mountain

There is something about the open road at sunset
That opens the door wide for my heart's wild,
Magical expression.

The in-between,

Leaving one time in place for another,
Except this one hasn't arrived yet.
Liminal space is my container for wonder,
imagination, and dreams—

Most importantly my dreams.

Promises

The only promise I will ever make.
What I express is only for that day.
Tomorrow it will probably change.
I have been a thousand different women.[1]

---

[1] This last line is from "You've Been a Thousand Different Women," by Emory Hall in her book *Made of Rivers* (New York: Three Rivers, 2023).

Wish upon a Star

What changes energy?
And how do we move it?
Does the universe hold energy in place for
spontaneous moments to occur?
And what about the fated moments,
The ones that took years to align,

The ones that change the course of someone's
destiny?
How long does the universe hold the energy for
those moments?

Or is the energy constantly changing,
Shifting by choice and somehow,
In some mysterious way,
Always aligning in those fated moments?

I wanted to know.
I was curious.
How many moments of my life were already
planned?
Is everything fated, or does free will play a part?

And if so, how much?

When I look at the stars,
I can't help but dream and believe,
That somehow the energy is fated,
Aligned in some magnetic way
That we will always end up exactly where we
are meant to be.

Moon Line

I wondered
How many lives I would live in this lifetime,
How many women I would choose to become,
All the lovers I would choose to love,
All the places I would discover.
I wondered.

What if I Just Farted in This Cafe?

The waitress was watching me.
A couple was enjoying a romantic meal to my
right.

I farted anyway

And continued singing along with Dolly Parton's
"Islands in the Stream":
"From one lover to another, ah-ha."
I looked back at the waitress.

She was still watching me.

She Moves

Dancing in the *shala*,
Butterflies for days,
Here, I belong.

Queen of Cups

I was waiting in line at the boarding gate.
For some reason, the airline hadn't assigned
me a seat number.
As I approached the woman at the desk,

I decided to try something I had never done
before.

I nervously asked, "Are there by chance any
upgrades on this flight?"

She kindly looked back at me and said,
"You know it's funny that you ask.
I just had to move someone for the group
that was ahead of you. There is an upgrade
available.
I can definitely move you up."

I was so squeaky inside with excitement.

Boarding the plane,
I took my seat next to a woman about my
mother's age.

She told me she was from Australia.
Normally, I am not an airplane seat chatter,

But this time was different.

I shared about my career,
Where I was headed, and the books and podcasts I enjoyed.
At one point the woman gently turned to me,
Looked me softly in the eyes, and said,

"You know, there are good people in the world, Taylor."

My whole body exhaled.
Tears started streaming down my face.
She could see me—really see me.
She reached over and wrapped her arms around me,

And I let her.

Springtime

Seven years ago,
The Irish Sea left a message.
Grief had captured my heart.
The message lost in the storm.
She came knocking once again,
Blooming in the nick of time.

My heart remembering her original call,
This time, I eagerly answered.

"An offering," she whispered,
"Is waiting exactly where you left it.
I see that you are afraid.
You have hidden the most precious parts of you.

"Don't you remember, sweet love,
Your divine makeup
Rests in the color blue?

"Dare to dive into my waters.
I promise you will do me no harm.
Allow this opening to release you.
The sunflowers, sweet love,
Have been waiting to shine through.

Dagda, the Divine Masculine

You were the first to arrive,
Leading me to County Donegal.

I sat in your fort for hours,
The stony palace of the sun.

Barefoot in the grass,
I opened my arms wide,

The good god, father of the Tuatha Dé Danann,
Your masculine strength, circling around me.

All my armor fell.

Stepping to the top of your palace,
I touched each stone along the way,
Sending you my heart's deepest desires.

On this early morning in May,

You told me there was no need to worry:
I was exactly where I was meant to be.

Adventure is in your heart, my love.
You are already well on your way.

Your soul a brave one indeed.
I am applauding you answered the call.

Continue to follow your tameless spirit.
I will be right here when you need.
I have no doubts about you, my love.

It is time you learn to receive.

Brigid's Love

My withered bones met the soil.
Your flame rested at my hips.
Green, luscious grass.
The golden daffodils were left as an offering.
Your cross placed gently to the north.
My body was welcomed by your warm embrace,
This holy well overflowing
With nourishment, abundance, and fertility.

Spring is peeking through.
My aching heart is resting safely here with you.

Rhythm

Three women,
One drum circle.
In the mountains,
Under the stars,
My heart beats to the rhythm.
She honors the journey.

Pisces Dreamer

I am howling at the moon.
She is full, expressing herself in Pisces,
Mystical,
The night sky holding her dear.
Off in the distance,
Tiny lights shine from the houses on the mountain.
I smile.
Curiosity never escapes me, and I am so grateful.

Three of Cups

I signed up to attend a women's retreat to
practice feeling my feelings in groups.
One-on-one feelings, I was your woman
(Most of the time).

Group feelings?
Absolutely terrified me
(All the time).

My higher self told me this would be a good
opportunity for growth.
I was in the business of listening to her these
days,
So I signed up.
I even selected to have a roommate.

I was all in.

A few of us gathered by the swimming pool.
Some were already in the pool, casually chatting,
While others were enjoying the sun in the lounge
chairs.
As I stepped onto what I thought was the initial
first step,

I realized a beat too late that there wasn't a step.
I fell in, splashing the other women in the pool.

When I gathered myself,
Feeling very confused and full of embarrassment,
I caught a glimpse of a small sign located on a fence about waist high next to a patio table.

It read, "Please enter the pool from the other side."

I started laughing and commented to my roommate:
"You know, they really should put that sign somewhere you can see it."
She laughed out loud.
Wiping my face, I thought, *If this isn't a metaphor for my entire existence,
I don't know what is.*

Dear Seattle

I spent hours in the window nook
Overlooking the harbor,
That tiny apartment

Holding so much of you,

The words filling the pages.
I had never felt more like me,

Effortless.

Acoustic guitar strings filled the room,
My toes tapping in tune.

I noticed a couple walking with a stroller.
Here, it felt so real.
The morning sun was peeking through.
"One day," my heart whispered.
"For now, it's just me and you."

Pathways

My boots hit the trail,
My breath meeting the desert air,
The morning sun peeking through.
I discover a cutie stream along the way.
Finding water in the desert makes me giggle.
It reminds me that nothing is an accident—
And I mean nothing.

Her Voice

She whispered, "Descend."
I tried to bargain instead.
She laughed, amused.
"It's time, love," she spoke gently.

Naked, I dove in.

An emerald gown, glitter, and gold.
One single braid.
The top of my head.
My eyes opened wide.
A crown, the melody.
My hands to the keys.

Remember, love?

Microphones

I bought myself a portable pink karaoke machine as a way to show up for my little self.

We had a relationship to repair, and I was determined to let her know that she was the light of my life.

When I opened the box, the machine glowed.

My cheeks hurt from the giant smile plastered across my face.

Every day, I would hold performances in my living room, bedroom, and kitchen, allowing her full self-expression.

One day, I called my friend and said,

"It's time for the next step. I'm ready for karaoke with people."

He laughed. "Definitely count me in."

I walked into the bar, spoke with the DJ, and added my name to the list.

When it was my turn, I walked to the center of the room, grabbed the microphone, and looked up at the TV.

"Wannabe" by the Spice Girls appeared on the top of the screen.

I gave it everything I had and even included some dance moves I felt were necessary.

When the last few beats of the song were playing, I paused.

The entire room was cheering my name.

I quickly turned to my left, my eyes wide, and looked at my friend, who was clapping and nodding his head yes.

I wasn't wearing a minidress with platform boots, but I was wearing a crop top without a bra, and for me,

I was communicating the same message.

Taking my seat at the table, I heard my little self whisper,

"Thank you."

I whispered back, "Anytime, babe. Anytime."

Curtains

I felt different.
I noticed
Patterns, behaviors, subtleties.
I couldn't place it.

The lack of love.
The lack of love.

Don't we all want the same thing?

I felt out of place.
Couldn't they see?
I stepped farther back.
This wasn't the place for my heart to be seen.

I started searching
For the people and places
Who felt like me,
Hearts wide open,
Hands held and free.

I stepped forward.
Now they would see.

Ghosts

I was dancing with your ghost
At two o'clock in the morning, candlelight, guitar
strings.
You wouldn't let me go.

The wood floor creaked beneath my bare feet.
Your sweater against my skin.

Evergreen.
We met in the space between.

I dreamt of the countryside, cobblestones
Tangled in the sunrise, your sleepy face.

Would you meet me here?

The Five Senses

I began exploring my body, my sensuality, and
my sexuality without another being present,
With the question, how can I receive pleasure
from myself alone?

I started doing everything naked.

I stood in front of my mirror naked.
Naked cooking.
Naked yoga.
Naked dancing.
Naked swimming.
I sat on my couch strumming my guitar naked.
I set a cold grape in my belly button.
I giggled.
It rolled out.

Over time, I slowly involved other beings in a
nonphysical way.

I attended a weekly slow and sexy dance class.
In one of the classes,
The teacher taught the class how to twerk.

Chairs were involved.
My body screamed, *Yes!*

So, I continued listening to her.

I joined a local pole studio.
Took pottery classes.
Zip-lined down a mountain.
Took ballet classes.
Indoor skydived.
Bit into an orange and let the juice squirt all over
my mouth.
My whole face scrunched.
So juicy.

Every day I began asking myself,

What do you need from me?
How can I give you pleasure?

Whispers

Drumbeats under the stars,
My heart wide open.
The uncharted territory
So buzzy, but ah, to be free!
I walked the path
Through the darkness
Amid the forest trees.
I discovered nature's ecstasy.
"Look up," she whispered.
"I am here to set you free."

Window Seats

I wondered,
Were the humans coming or going?
Loving or longing?
Here, my heart felt free,
Boundless, wild, full of magic.
She held stories
Of dragons, knights, and castles.
"The mermaids," my heart whispered.

"Of course," I whispered back.
My head rested on the window edge.
Here, my heart felt free.

Fires

Was this OK?
Permission.
If not that, then this?
Speak.
No, not like that.
Force. Flames.
It's too much?
A little softer.
Whisper.
No, louder.
I thought I was too loud?
Permission.

Earth School Hits Me in
All the Tender Places

When you stop controlling yourself to make the
room comfortable,
When you stop making decisions based on
what's best for others

And start making decisions based on what is
best for you,

When you stop settling and accepting less than
you deserve,
When you stop holding yourself back to maintain
a relationship,
When you stop taking responsibility for the
actions of others

And start taking responsibility for yourself,

When your knowing says your current container
is too small,
When your knowing says you need to leave a
relationship, job, or place of residence,

Are you brave enough to listen?

When you realize the music was inside you all
along,
When you realize your power reaches to the
highest of galaxies,
When you realize you were meant to lead and
not follow,
When you realize a partnership, child, or job will
never define you,

How will you define yourself?

Hourglass

Waves crashing, my heart bursting.
The ache, persistent.

It was always there.

Holding and soothing,
Numbing and running,

It was always there.

I was torn
Between remembering and knowing,
Loving and longing.
The end was near
For you and me.

The unspoken hung in the air.

Boulders

I resisted the whole way.
Autonomy, sovereignty,
I demanded to express.
She loved me anyway,
Softly, quietly, in whispers.

I Say Hello to Improv

Being funny is my little self's all-time favorite
activity.
She loves laughing, and she loves making other
people laugh too.
She loves being outrageous and unfiltered,
owning the entire room.
Her mind is quick, zipping around like the
scrambler ride at the county fair.
She loves stages.
And people.
Definitely microphones.
There is a special kind of magic that happens
on a stage when a group of people are gathered
together:
A new creation, feeling, idea, inspiration.
Art in any form, she craves it.
I decided to attend a local improv jam.
As a small step, I told all my parts that we would
participate in the warm-ups but that we could
save the skits for another time.
I walked onto the small stage and stood in the
circle.
I loved being in circles.

I made noises, passed energy, created sentences, chanted, and laughed at myself a lot.

Improv required a vulnerability and confidence I admired.

The following week, I participated in the short and long form skits.

The week after that, I signed up for the classes. As I left the studio, closing the door behind me, I thought,

This story is only just beginning.

Breath

To live among the flowers,
Delicate, wild, and free.
I never wanted to leave.
Breath.
I could breathe here.
My whole body expanded.
Sensual loving touch.
To live among the flowers.
I never wanted to leave.

Depth

She always made me feel,
The ocean.
Her waves soothed me,
Understood me.
I felt seen
And held.
Leaving her left me exposed, raw.
The ocean,
She always made me feel.

My Thoughts on Stormy Days

Were we all playing out the same wounds?
Feminine and masculine,

A perceived lack,
A distorted perception.

We couldn't see each other.
The space between felt foggy, unseen.

But wasn't that where the magic was?
Why were we choosing weapons
When there was a greater space to hold,

An abundance, readily available,
Of light, freedom, and air?

Here, take my hand.
We can walk this path together,
I looking out for you,
You looking out for me.

It's OK if you stumble.
I know I will fall too.
I will be right here if you need me.
If you reach,
I will reach out for you.

Once upon a Time

I was sitting in the cafe
Window seat, a warm cup of tea in my hand
Surrounded in emerald.

My eyes met the castle.
Dreaming of you and me.

The ballroom, purple velvet.
The small of my back held by your hand.
My eyes locked with yours.

Two heartbeats
Harmonizing,
Dancing with the flower moon
In a crowded room.

It was only you and me.

Will You Still Hold Me?

When I don't fall in line,
When I have something to say—

Dissent—

When I don't believe
And lose all hope,
When my light is dim
And the tears fall,
When my body meets the ground
My hands filled with despair,

Will you still hold me?

I Took a Peek and Found Samples

I had always been a commitment girl.
Lately, I was challenging the word *always*.
Had I really always been a commitment girl?
I had spent the majority of my teens and twenties
in and out of some form of relationship with a
few casual dating exceptions.
I decided to ask my heart one morning.
She replied, "Dude, you also like samples.
You like the idea of commitment with the right
person, but you definitely like samples. Maybe
try that for a spin."
My heart was right.
I was way too curious not to love samples.
I loved food samples:
City samples,
Music samples,
Weather samples,
Samples of people,
Job samples—hella job samples—
You name it.
I was most definitely a sampler.
I took my heart's advice along with the mantra,
"Curiosity does not mean commitment."

We met at the lake during sunset.

A man was playing his acoustic guitar nearby.

His outfit communicated effort, and I smiled.

The wine bar where we planned to grab a drink was closed.

"The store is right there. What do you say we grab a bottle and sit by the lake?" I suggested.

"That's a good idea. Or if you feel comfortable, we can walk back to my place. I have a few good options. Absolutely no pressure," he said gently.

He was a mind reader.

Oddly enough, I felt completely comfortable to accept his invitation.

"Let's do it," I said, smiling, linking my left arm through his right.

My whole intention for this date was to have a one-night stand.

I was exploring all things sample and sensual.

The universe was delivering.

Back at his place, we split a bottle of red

And talked for more than four hours,

My feet draped over his lap on the couch,

Listening to John Mayer, laughing, and sharing personal stories.

I felt as if I had known him forever.

He too had grown up in the Midwest and had ventured elsewhere,
In search of something other than what he knew.
I vulnerably shared, "I'm still figuring out this whole body thing and exploring my sexuality."
He genuinely replied, "Oh, me too. I struggle with being comfortable in my body. It's getting better, but it's definitely still something I'm working on."
"Really?" I asked softly.
"That was really sweet of you to share that with me," I said graciously.
"Yeah, of course. I feel like I can talk to you about anything," he said.
I smiled.
"You think the whole body issue is a Midwest thing, or what?" I joked
He laughed. "Yeah, that's definitely part of it."
"Want to know something?" I asked.
"Definitely," he replied.

"My whole intention for this night was to have a one-night stand with you."

He laughed. "Oh, really? Have you had one before?"

"Nope," I replied. "Are you going to be OK if I never talk to you again after this?" I laughed.

"Well, I'd be lying if I said I wasn't going to be bummed. I've never met anyone like you before. You're really cool, but I'm definitely not saying no to you either." He smiled.

We both laughed.

The next morning, he brought me coffee in bed and rearranged his work schedule so he could drive me back to my apartment.

"Thanks for not making me do the whole walk-of-shame thing," I joked as I leaned over to kiss him goodbye.

"I would never," he said back. "I know this would ruin your whole one-night stand adventure, but I'd love to see you again if you're up for it. You have my number."

I smiled and gave him my best wink, and as I closed the passenger door of his truck, I thought,

Midwestern guys are the absolute best.

Music Notes

I need you.
Do you see?
Ballet shoes
Falling across the wood floor,
Arms flowing,

The sea moving with me
And in me,

Held so gently
And free.

The butterflies knew.

Speckled yellow,
The backdrop faded.
Her wings spread wide,
She rested on my palm,

Open,

My arms flowing,
Falling across the wood floor.

Do you see?

Hello, Bee, It's Me

Thousands had gathered to admire the cliffs.
Indeed, their beauty captivating.
Crowds gathered, cameras flashing.
I found myself wandering to the wildflowers,
Lightly touching their yellow petals.

Curious, I noticed

A small bee making herself cozy next to me.
"Hello, bee, it's me."
She giggled.
"I like your wings," I whispered.

"I like yours too," she whispered back.

Strength

Her pain filled my body.
I held it
As an act of courage.

Self-harm.
The invisible
Became known,

An undoing
Only Mother Nature could hold.

The leaves turned gold,
Eventually dancing through the air,
The snow bustling in.
Shivers inside my bones.
Spring whispered hello,
Her flowers in full bloom.
The summer sun gave voice

To all that bled through.

Her Siren Song

Allow time to unfold.
Allow the truth to be told.
Lightning strikes,
The dark seas rise.
My head resting softly on my pillow.
Goodnight sweet moon.

Sophia

Once upon a time,
An outdated jacket,
A gift she once gave me.
Years went by,
My body screaming,
"Not this! Not this!"
I looked around,
Afraid to take off the jacket.
She liked me better this way.
My mind lost in Neverland,
The magic, fairies, and wonder.
My eyes opened wide.
"Here you don't have to wear that jacket.
Take my hand. I'll show you," he said.
I carefully slipped one arm out
And then another,
The cool breeze hitting my skin.
I gently set the jacket down.
Unsteady, I looked over at him.
He smiled. "You have never looked more
like you."
My whole body exhaled.
"Are you ready? They're waiting for you."

Printed in the United States
by Baker & Taylor Publisher Services